Mann

The Inspirational Story of Baseball Superstar Manny Machado

Table Of Contents

Introduction

As the title already implies, this is a short book about [The Inspirational Story of Baseball Superstar Manny Machado] and how he rose from his life in Miami, Florida to becoming one of today's leading and most-respected baseball players. In his rise to superstardom, Manny has inspired not only the youth, but fans of all ages, throughout the world.

This book also portrays the key moments that Manny has had to go through during his early childhood years, his teen years, and up until he became what he is today. A notable source of inspiration is Manny's service to the community and his strong connection with the fans of the sport. He continues to serve as the humble, hard-working superstar in a sport that needs positive role models.

Combining incredible strength, a strong throwing arm, high baseball IQ, and superior coordination, Manny has shown the ability to change the outcome of any game. From playing catch with his uncle to becoming one of the greatest young ball players of his generation, you'll learn here how this man has risen to the ranks of the best baseball players today.

Thanks again for grabbing this book. Hopefully you can take some of the examples from Manny's story and apply them to your own life!

Chapter 1:

Childhood & Family Life

On July 6th, 1992 the world welcomed Manuel Arturo Machado. Manny was born as the second child to his mother, Rosa Nunez. Born and raised in the inner city of Miami, Florida, Manny was lucky to have his uncle, Geovanny Brito, available to help him develop as a baseball player. His uncle lived across the street and would teach Manny about life and the game of baseball whenever he had free time.

Because his mother was a single mother who had to work multiple jobs to make ends meet, Manny learned to really appreciate the meaning of family. His aunts, uncles, and grandparents all played a part in raising Manny into a man who has morals and stays out of trouble. Because of this strong support system, he was able to avoid many of the pitfalls that come with being raised in an inner-city urban environment.

As Manny developed into a young boy, he and his uncle began to traditionally play toss in the front of Geovanny's home. This continued until Manny was old enough to play in little league baseball tournaments. Manny's passion and desire for the game of baseball sprung from this relationship with his uncle.

Another key family member in Manny's development was his grandfather, Francisco Nunez. Francisco taught Manny many lessons that he learned over the years, including getting through to Manny about the significance of remaining humble throughout his journey in life. Even though Francisco passed away just before Manny was able to play his first major league game, Manny was able to soak up the wisdom and has internalized his grandfather's spirit as part of his own.

Manny remembers watching Opening Day games on the television with his grandfather each year. To this day, Manny sketches the letters "F.N." into the infield dirt, the initials of his late grandfather. Francisco is essentially with Manny each time he makes a spectacular play out there on the baseball diamond.

Manny went on to attend Brito High School in Miami and starred on the baseball team. This was where he really started to physically develop and fill out his frame, while also mentally maturing as a star player that could come through in clutch moments of the game.

During his youth, Manny was able to hang out with an older crowd, as his sister was eight years older than he was. These experiences helped Manny to mature quickly and understand how to not embarrass himself in front of others, even if he was the youngest in the room.

He played baseball and basketball throughout his youth, but basketball was not his passion and Manny realized that he had natural abilities and inclinations to excel on the baseball field from an early age.

One of Manny's childhood idols was Alex Rodriguez, the superstar slugger who played for the Mariners, Rangers, and New York Yankees.

Manny admired his swagger and charisma, not to mention his incredible play-making abilities on the defensive side of the ball, to go along with his world-class power at the plate.

Chapter 2:

Professional Life

During his high school years, Manny worked extremely hard to become the best player that he could, essentially separating himself from the pack. By the time he was a senior in high school, Manny was ranked as the second best high school position player in the graduating class of 2010. As a result, the Baltimore Orioles chose Manny with the third overall selection in the 2010 MLB Draft. He was initially signed to a $5.25 million contract and publicly introduced by the Orioles in mid-September.

Minor Leagues

In August of 2010, Manny was assigned to play in the Gulf Coast League for the Baltimore Orioles' minor league affiliate team. As a designated hitter, Manny got his professional career started off on the Class-A team, Aberdeen IronBirds. Eventually he was put at the shortstop position and showed that he had the athleticism and control to play the position.

He was later moved to Class-A Delmarva Shorebirds and began to show potential when he hit five home runs within the first few weeks of play. His momentum continued and he was eventually selected to the 2012 All-Star Futures Game, a game which features the rising stars in the minor leagues in hopes to showcase their talent.

Baltimore Orioles

2012

At the beginning of the 2012 season, Orioles management decided to move Manny up from the Class-AA level to play for the Orioles in the majors. In his second major league game, Manny hit two home runs, becoming the youngest Oriole to have a multi-home run game. An interesting aside about his multiple home run game was the fact that the same fan caught both balls.

Manny continued to impress during his rookie season in the big leagues, as he had an above-average year on both offense and defense. He showed flashes of brilliance and potential, driving balls deep out of the park and robbing opposing hitters of base hits on multiple occasions.

Manny was able to get his first career postseason home run in the 2012 American League Division Series, however the Orioles would eventually lose the series to the New York Yankees in only five games.

2013

It didn't take long for Manny to find himself in legendary company, when by the end of May, he broke Ty Cobb's record for the most multi-hit games before the age of 21, with 41. Furthermore, Manny went on to put himself into the record books with another legend, when he recorded 44 hits in the month of May, the second most by a player under the age of 21, since Mickey Mantle had 46 hits in July of 1952.

Obviously with all of the legendary company, Manny was having a breakout season. So much so, that by the end of May, he was leading the entire Majors with twenty five doubles and was in a tie with Miguel Cabrera for the most hits, at 79. He was recognized for his great effort by the midway point of the season, being voted in as an All-Star for the American League team.

Unfortunately, in a regular season game following the All-Star break, Manny suffered a knee injury while running past first base. He was taken off the field in a stretcher and it was a big emotional loss for the Orioles team and fan base. Also, the injury forced Manny to end his consecutive games streak at 207. Nevertheless, Manny was able to put up solid numbers in his second season with the Orioles and showed the world that he would be a force to be reckoned with in years to come.

Especially noteworthy was the fact that Manny looked like a veteran out there on the defensive side of the ball. He led the entire American League in fielding percentage at third base - an extremely impressive feat for someone who was as young as he was.

For his great season, Manny was awarded the Gold Glove Award, following in the footsteps of Oriole legend Brooks Robinson. To top it off, he also was awarded the Platinum Glove Award, an honor given to the best overall fielder in the majors. Manny underwent reconstructive surgery for his knee and looked to recover fully for the 2014 campaign.

2014

By the end of April 2014, Manny was cleared to play and was subsequently removed from the Orioles' disabled list. His return went as expected, receiving a standing ovation from the Baltimore faithful in his first home game back. Before long, Manny was back to form, making stellar plays at third base and he even hit his first career grand slam against the Houston Astros.

Unfortunately, just as Manny was gaining momentum and confidence in his game, he suffered another injury to his knee, this time to the right one. During an at-bat in a game against the New York Yankees, Manny appeared to tweak his knee in an awkward position. It was later announced that he would require surgery and miss the remainder of the 2014 season.

Scouting Report on Manny

It is no secret amongst respected opinions in the league, that Manny Machado is one of the most-talented third basemen to come into Major League Baseball in the last decade. Despite his young age and boyish face, Manny has shown that he has natural instincts that even veteran players struggle to learn after years of practice. Whether it is the strength of his arm, the range he can cover with his feet, or just the intuitive, on-the-spot decisions that Manny makes, such as when he faked a throw to first, only to turn around and catch a runner cheating off of third base - any team in the Majors would love to have him covering their corner.

As a player profile, it is no surprise that Manny has drawn comparisons to Alex Rodriguez, the player that Manny views as his mentor. Not only does Manny have an impressive build and quick feet, but his willingness to play the position instinctively allows him to make plays that other players may not be willing to try. Among other comparisons are Cal Ripken Jr. and Brooks Robinson, two former Orioles' greats who showed the star potential that Manny possesses.

At the plate, Manny is surprisingly patient and has shown that he does not get visibly intimidated by opposing pitchers. He sticks with his routine and tries to keep things as simple as possible. If you watch him during the clutch moments of a game, you will notice that he never lets the magnitude of a moment get to him.

Chapter 3:

Personal Adult Life

Despite the immense superstardom that Manny has found himself in, he is still just a young man in his early twenties who has most of the same hobbies as other people his age. His favorite musician is Jay-Z and he loves to gobble down Philly cheesesteaks when he gets the chance. He also loves to play video games in his free time, most notably NBA2K.

He still loves his mom as much as he did when he was a child and he has even found a woman who he is fond enough to be engaged to, by the name of Yainee Alonso. Yainee is the younger sister of Yonder Alonso, the first baseman for the San Diego Padres. Manny met Yainee through

Yonder, as the two were friends when Manny was a senior in high school and Yonder was playing at the University of Miami.

They developed a strong friendship as they worked out together in the same gym in Miami. Ever since then, Yonder has played the big brother role and has helped Manny adjust both mentally and physically to the life of a professional baseball player.

Speaking of adjusting to the new life, Manny now drives a black Porsche, a fact that he doesn't boast or brag about. Any young man in a similar position would treat himself to a new car, but the generous person that Manny is really shines through in his ability to take care of those he loves. With the money he has earned in his young career so far, Manny has already bought his mother a house. He is happier about this accomplishment than anything that he has done for himself.

Manny has reached celebrity status and is especially a big hit with the young ladies who are baseball fans, as his youthful look and innocence is something that not many star players have. Because he has been able to keep his head on straight and not fall into the trap of believing in his own hype, he remains a likable personality to fans and serves as a great ambassador for the sport.

As a side note, Manny has also mentioned that he has a few tattoos. These include two stars on his hands, one picture of his grandfather, and another of his favorite animal, a lion.

Chapter 4:

Philanthropic/Charitable Acts

In Manny's short time in Baltimore, he has already become a fan favorite who enjoys having a strong connection with the community. He has attended multiple charity events as a participant and has even created his own way of giving back.

Along with the help of the Baltimore City Foundation, Manny decided to hold his own charity event. His idea was to create a bowling event to raise funds for the Baltimore City Recreation and Parks. Proceeds would help the summer program for nine to twelve year old children.

It was called the "BaseBowl" celebrity bowling tournament, featuring many of his teammates and coaches who were partnered into teams to play two full games. Following the games, there was a silent auction to go along with a dinner. It turned out to be a very effective event and Manny was able to serve as a catalyst for something that would change the lives of many children in the Baltimore area.

The funny part about Manny choosing to host a bowling tournament, is that Manny is not particularly a great bowler, as he has admitted. He joked that he just hoped to score in the triple digits. Furthermore, the event was able to incorporate sponsors who paid as low as $5,000 all the way to $25,000 to share the lanes with Manny and his teammates.

The funds raised for these children helped to provide them with transportation, equipment, and even uniforms that they could wear for practice and in games.

Chapter 5:

Legacy, Potential & Inspiration

Manny's young career has just started and he still has a lot more to accomplish. However, he already has pressure to live up to and has inspired millions of people around the world.

Most notably, his presence in the line-up brings joy to the people of Baltimore. There was an obvious feeling of sadness around the stadium during the time of Manny's injuries and a noticeable rush of happiness when he returned. He has helped to rejuvenate a franchise that is sometimes mocked for not experiencing any success since the days of Cal Ripken Jr. and Brooks Robinson.

However, the city of Baltimore has become enthusiastic about it's team once again. Not only have they become serious playoff contenders in the past few years, but even players who have been around, such as Adam Jones, have noted that since the new faces of Machado and manager Buck Showalter, there is genuine belief within the fan base.

Conclusion

I hope this book was able to help you gain inspiration from the life of Manny Machado, one of the best players currently playing in Major League Baseball.

The rise and fall of a star is often the cause for much wonder. But most stars have an expiration date. In baseball, once a star player reaches his mid- to late-thirties, it is often time to contemplate retirement. What will be left in people's minds about that fading star? In Manny Machado's case, people will remember how he came onto the scene for the Orioles and became an instant fan favorite. He will be remembered as the guy who helped his team resurrect their image in the chase to a championship, while building his own image along the way.

Manny has also inspired so many people because he is the star who never fails to connect with fans and give back to the less fortunate. Noted for his ability to impose his will on any game, he is a joy to watch on the baseball field. Last but not least, he's remarkable for remaining simple and firm with his principles in spite of his immense popularity. Quiet, laid-back, and shy, this Baltimore Orioles third baseman has baseball fans in awe with a playing prowess that sportswriters say is comparable to that of the legendary, Cal Ripken Jr.

Hopefully you've learned some great things about Manny in this book and are able to apply some of the lessons that you've learned to your own life! Good luck in your journey!

41202146R00020

Made in the USA
Middletown, DE
04 April 2019